Eastbourne
in old picture postcards

Tony Wales

European Library ZALTBOMMEL/THE NETHERLANDS

Acknowledgements:

Cecil Cramp for his unfailing help at all times. Also John Cannon, Martin Graebe and John Payne. And in particular Martin Hayes and Robin Knibb of the West Sussex Library Service for the following pictures: Numbers 1, 41 and 66.

Bibliography:

Adamson, S.H: Seaside Piers. 1977.

Armstrong, Robert: The Beachy Head Light. (ND)

Boylett, Lionel J: Eastbourne Tramways. (ND)

Chapman, Bridgid: East Sussex Inns. 1988.

Gautry, A: Some Eastbourne Folk of Bygone days. 1978.

Hodges, Peter R.: Temples of Dreams. 1994.

Morris, Jeff and Dave Hendy: The Story of the Eastbourne Lifeboats. 1988.

Ogley, Bob; Ian Currie and Mark Davison: The Sussex Weather Book. 1991.

Reed, T: The Fishermen and Boatmen of Eastbourne. 1975.

Spears, H.D.: Some of the Street Names of Eastbourne. 1975.

Spears, H.D.: The stream that gave Eastbourne its name. 1975.

Stevens, Lawrence: A Short History of Eastbourne. 1991.

BACK IN TIME

European Library

post office box 49

NL – 5300 AA Zaltbommel/The Netherlands

telephone: 0031 418 513144

fax: 0031 418 515515

e-mail: publisher@eurobib.nl

Introduction

Eastbourne has often been portrayed as everyone's ideal holiday resort, and indeed this may not be very far from the truth. It is clean and tidy, with good beaches, an enviable climate most of the time, and very little to disturb either the holidaymakers or the residents.

Some of the titles bestowed on the town over the years, give a good idea of what Eastbourne aims at, and usually achieves: 'The Empress of Watering Places', 'The Town of Trees' (it once boasted of 10,000 of these), and even 'The Naples of Sussex' are some of the descriptive names that have been used. It has even been suggested that it is the modern embodiment of the ancient Sussex 'Anderida'. The town's official motto 'Let us follow better things' may be rendered in modern parlance as 'Beautiful Healthy Eastbourne'.

Like many other coastal resorts Eastbourne originated in a modest settlement. This was known as Burne, which later became Bourne. Here was a chalk stream, which was until quite modern times an overflow from a nearby pond. Close-by were the withy beds used by local basket makers. (Once a local man was fined for driving his pigs into the pond.) Subsequently the prefix East was added, probably to distinguish it from another town with a similar name. Growth was rapid. By 1780 it was described as 'a desirable watering place', when the children of George III came to the town and stayed for four months. By 1911 it had become a County Borough and one can say that progress has continued ever since, with a population of 1,668 at the start of the nineteenth century, which shot up to 52,544 by the start of the twentieth.

Mr. G.R. Sims writing at the latter time said: 'The white, stony glare which in other seaside towns is so distressing is here conspicuous by its absence... Many of the busiest thoroughfares would console a Parisian for the loss of his beloved boulevards.'

Unlike some other seaside towns Eastbourne has always aimed at quality, rather than attempting to emulate towns such as Brighton or Hastings with their attractions for day trippers. This has inevitably led to a few unkind remarks aimed at Eastbourne, usually to the effect that many of the residents and visitors are elderly and sleepy. Unkind folk have remarked that the town has no young folk to pick up the many old folk when they fall down. (It was even said that the seagulls were taught to fly upside down to keep the promenades clean, and that shop-keepers provided bi-focal windows.) Certainly the town had a policy of no hawkers, musicians or donkeys, and there was a good living to be had out of hiring out bath chairs at one and six an hour. But scoffers could not prevent Eastbourne from becoming a beautifully clean and congenial holiday town for all those who looked for something better than a mere hasty look at the sea, and a fish and chip supper. Recommendations, if such were needed, came from the many celebrities who chose to stay in the town through the years. These included Tennyson, Blackmore, Gissing, Debussy and Darwin. The latter stayed in a house in Marine Parade, whilst working on his 'The Origin of Species' in the 1850s. Professor T.H. Huxley built a house here, and Richard Jefferies conceived his famous work 'The Story of my Heart' whilst staying at nearby Pevensey. Another regular visitor was Lewis Carroll, who spent his summers in Lushington Road. Friedrich Engels, collaborator of Karl Marx, often holidayed at Eastbourne, and when he died in 1895 his ashes were scattered off Beachy Head. Trees and flowers have always played a major part in the face which Eastbourne presents to its visitors. A guide book from the beginning of the twentieth century noted: 'The slopes between the parades are planted with tamarisk and a number of flowers that change with the seasons – wallflowers in spring, poppies, cornflowers and evening primroses in the summer and autumn. Such a floral display in proximity to the sea is picturesque in the extreme.' Coming forward to the year 2000 a modern guide-book says much the same in different words: 'The beautiful sea-front gardens capture the elegance of Victorian bedding and floral sculpture. A new bedding display is set out each year.'

In this present book we look back at Eastbourne's recent past, from the end of the nineteenth century to the middle of the twentieth. May you, the reader, find these old pictures fascinating and rewarding.

1 This is Eastbourne at the turn of the centuries from the 19th to the twentieth. It had already laid claim to being the most fashionable seaside resort in Sussex, and was developing rapidly under the principle land-owner the Duke of Devonshire.

The seafront extended for three miles, with roads and paths at different levels, with, in the distance the famous Beachy Head, with its chalk cliff 575 feet high. This fine panoramic photo was the work of G. and R. Lavis of Eastbourne.

2   Another picture soon after the same period, but this time a print, well embellished with fashionably dressed visitors and lots of activity both on the promenade and the beach.

At this time the Burlington Hotel, looking suitably staid and respectable, is central to the seafront. Other hotels at this period were The Cavendish, The Claremont, The Queensborough, The Alexandra and The Mayfair. Typical tariffs were single rooms four shillings; double rooms seven and sixpence, with a full week's board seventy-three shillings and sixpence.

According to a guide book of the period, behind the seafront hotels were 'shops that might have been transposed bodily from the most fashionable part of London'.

3   The year is 1904 and we are thoroughly 'down to earth' with a message on a postcard, which reads: 'Expect me home tomorrow night at the usual time.' The six people arranged so neatly on the front of the card are part of the Cramp family on holiday from Horsham. (Another member of the family took the photo.) The boat they are using as a back-drop was one of many such craft which beguiled holiday-makers with the promise of 'a trip round the light-house'. If the tide was right they might even be allowed to actually land on the rocks which surrounded the light house.

4   This picture of the beach dates from around 1920. Eastbourne had a good beach for boats, with its slight shelving. Rowing boats could be hired for one shilling and sixpence for the first hour, and sailing boat fares could be as little as five shillings. As at many other seaside resorts, Eastbourne had its favourite sailing boat 'The Skylark'. No hawkers were allowed on the beach, but the fishermen had been there since at least the seventeenth century, with surnames such as Tutt, Erridge, Bodle and Bartholomew. Eastbourne fishermen were known as 'willock-eaters' (willocks were guillemots, who's flesh is very unpalatable).

PIER & BEACH, EASTBOURNE.

5   Coming forward to 1951 with this busy picture of holidaymakers enjoying the attractions provided for them on the beach. Just a few of the events in Eastbourne in the 1950s were three flower shows a year, Navy Week, County Cricket Week, a Carnival, a Regatta, a Croquet Tournament and an Angling Festival. Deck chairs could be hired for sixpence, and beach tents cost four pounds a month. There were two indoor swimming baths, as well as the expected sea cruises and motorboat trips.

6   This picture from about 1916 shows the busy scene at the Western Lawns on a typical Sunday morning, after church services. This regular weekly gathering of the brightest and best in their finery was known as 'The Church Parade', and was said to be the best place to find a wife or a husband. An 1899 newspaper reported: 'The Church Parade was a gay and animated scene, with some wonderful things in feminine attire to be seen.' By 1919 there were twenty-seven churches and chapels in Eastbourne, and this had increased to 32 by 1931.

E.46461. EASTBOURNE: CHURCH PARADE.

7 The period is around 1912 and the photo shows the large number of wheeled bathing machines which were in use at that time. These cabins, which were hauled out to the water by horses, were for several years managed by Mr. Fred Erridge, of a local fishing family. Ladies and gentlemen had separate machines in the early days and mixed bathing later caused a good deal of controversy (in 1922 bathing, bands and buses on Sundays, all caused a great deal of argument in the town). By 1930 the council were responsible for the bathing cabins, and they were hired out for sixpence per half hour (children fourpence). In 1935 Bathing Chalet No. 2 was used by King George V and Queen Mary on a holiday in Eastbourne. Also in this picture can be seen a small crowd enjoying a show at the beach theatre.

Beach, Grand Parade and Pier, Eastbourne, 531.

8 The Round House at Splash Point as seen on a painting about 1840. This was demolished in 1841 due to the buffeting it received from the sea. Before that time, hundreds of residents and visitors would come to gaze at the awe-inspiring sight of the waves dashing against the sea wall. Those who stood too close were drenched by the water, but appeared to enjoy the experience. Prince Edward stayed here in 1780, one of the many who looked upon the building as an essential part of Eastbourne. When it was finally removed, remains of a Roman villa came to light, and subsequently further Roman remains were found in 1848.

ROUND HOUSE, SPLASH POINT, EASTBOURNE. 1840.

9 A print of Eastbourne pier soon after it was opened in June 1870. It was designed by the most famous pier architect Eugenius Birch (1818-1884), who looked upon it as one of the finest of his creations. In the first season Mr. Wolfe's German Band played to appreciative audiences, with his company of twelve musicians, receiving £3 for their efforts, four times a day, seven days a week. When Mr. Wolfe moved on, the sixteen-piece Hanoverian Band performed twice daily, being paid £250 for the complete season from June to October.

For many years, Christmas morning early bathing from the pier was considered an essential part of the festive attractions.

10 An undated picture of the pier, in its heyday of around the 1920s. By this time there were many additional features, including a ballroom (built in 1925) and a theatre, which seated over a thousand people. Here Horatio Bottomley, of John Bull fame, made one of his famous speeches. Other famous folk also appeared, including Robertson Hare, Edith Evans, Clarkson Rose, Sandy Powell, Ivor Novello, Frankie Vaughan and Norman Wisdom.
In the 1940s a military demolition squad placed explosive devices during a performance at the pier theatre. Staff were given three days to prepare for complete demolition, although this was never actually carried out. However, the pier was subsequently damaged by enemy action.

Eastbourne.   The Pier Pavilion.

11   One of the many boats, which made use of the pier during the Summer seasons. (This was in 1951.) Sometimes there were as many as four a day, with no-passport-trips to Boulogne, starting after the Second World War; although these ceased in 1963.

At the height of the popularity for steamer trips, one could go from the pier to Brighton, Worthing, Hastings, Folkestone, the Isle of Wight, as well as France. The famous paddle steamer The Waverley also made use of the pier.

12 Charabancs on Eastbourne seafront about 1905. The charabancs had canvas hoods, which folded back in fine weather. If it rained, as of course it often did, the passengers were expected to help with re-erecting the hoods. By the 1920s, Chapman and Sons owned a large number of 'well appointed motor charabancs' and were running daily trips to various beauty spots in Sussex. The firm also ran an express service between Eastbourne and London, the single fare being eleven shillings. Their rivals the Southdown Company advertised with 'luxurious torpedo charabanc cars'.

Eastbourne.

Parade with Char-a-Banc Procession.

696.

13 One of Eastbourne's many bowling-greens; this was on Royal Parade about 1913. For many years bowls has been one of the most popular pastimes in the summer season, and by 1929 a bowling tournament was being held annually in Whit Week. In 1929 the cost of playing bowls on an Eastbourne Green was only twopence an hour, with a shilling for a whole day. By 1931 this had risen to eightpence an hour.

The ladies' hats in the foreground were typical of the period, when hats were considered one of the most important articles of female clothing.

Eastbourne, The Bowling Green, Royal Parade,   503

14 Eastbourne's Carpet Gardens about 1906. This is still one of the town's unique attractions, having been started over a century ago. The feature can claim to be 'world famous', with thousands of plants being used each year. Originally they were known simply as 'the flower beds', but an unknown genius quickly bestowed their present name upon them.

This is one of the many postcards showing the Carpet Gardens, which have been bought and posted by holidaymakers over the years. It was sent to London, but the message is rather an unkind one, as it says: 'There is nothing to do here this evening, so that is why I am writing to you.'

Eastbourne - Carpet Gardens.

15 The Redoubt Bandstand circa 1924. This cost nearly £10,000 to build, and stood to the west of the Redoubt Fort. The latter building was a fortress against Napoleon's men, and was completed about 1812. It was designed to hold 350 soldiers, although it is doubtful if it ever held that number. The Eastbourne Council took it over when the fort had become derelict and forlorn, and the building and the surrounding area were much improved
The crowd in this photo look rather less genteel than those seen on many Eastbourne pictures, but no doubt they thoroughly enjoyed the music.

REDOUBT BANDSTAND, EASTBOURNE.

16 The Wish Tower shown on a late nineteenth-century print. This is one of the Martello Towers built as a defence against the French in 1804. ('Wish' is an old word meaning 'a marshy place'.) It was based on a fort in Mortella Bay in Corsica, the word later corrupted to Martello. Napoleon had said: 'Let us be masters of the Channel for six hours, and we are masters of the world.' But he was deterred by twelve similar towers, along the south coast, manned by British soldiers armed with muskets – their efforts giving rise to such common expressions as 'Flash-in-the-pan' and 'Lock-stock-and-barrel'.

The fort was restored and opened to the public in May 1970, having been in turn Coast Guard quarters, and a private residence, following its original use by the military.

17   The Grand Hotel around 1906. This five-star-hotel, prior to the Second World War, was made famous by the wireless programme 'Grand Hotel' which featured the violinist Albert Sandler and his orchestra, which played regularly in 'The Palm Court'. Many celebrities have stayed here: Claude Debussy was a visitor in l905 with his mistress, and it was here that he completed the orchestration of his famous composition 'La Mer'. Lady Antonia Fraser and her husband Harold Pinter were two other celebrities who often stayed at the hotel.
The Grand advertised itself as 'The most celebrated hotel on the South Coast'.

Grand Hotel, Eastbourne.

18 Old Town circa 1910. As with many South Coast towns, the oldest part was perhaps once a slight embarrassment, with its out-of-date buildings, but has now become an interesting tourist attraction.

The census of 1841 showed that the old town was a veritable hive of local industry, with labourers, blacksmiths, tailors, drapers, butchers, cordwainers and hairdressers, as well as a vast number of other less common trades such as a strawbonnet maker, a sweep (and a sweep's boy) and perhaps surprisingly an accountant. Dare we mention it, but that old Sussex occupation of smuggling must also have been represented in the Old Town. This was particularly rife in the period around 1790, with fishermen supplementing their income by smuggling goods such as brandy, tobacco, tea, wine and silk. These men had unusual nicknames such as Killcraft, Alligators and Catseyes; names which persisted long after smuggling ceased.

THE OLD MANOR HOUSE AND HIGH STREET, OLD TOWN, EASTBOURNE.

19 Terminus Road circa 1914. This widely used road was once merely a footpath across open fields, until the railway station was built in 1849, and the road became one of the busiest thoroughfares in the town. This picture surprises by its lack of wheeled traffic, although someone has left a bicycle propped nonchalantly against a useful tree. Some of the young ladies are wearing straw 'boaters', so popular at this period. Pickfords and Hovis bread are two familiar names still with us today, although almost everything else has changed. The road is now partly dedicated to pedestrians and buses

Terminus Road, Eastbourne.

20 Mead's Road circa 1912. The Mead's area at the western end of the town was to quote an 1861 guide book: 'A small cluster of cottages and cornfields. About a quarter of a mile beyond South-bourne.' Then in the 1870s architect Henry Currey planned tree-lined streets of substantial Victorian style town houses, with several large villas. Since then it has been known as 'The Belgravia' of Eastbourne, celebrated for its pleasant character and picturesque buildings. To quote a 1930s guide book: 'In this locality are some of the best of the high class schools which are so prominent a feature of Eastbourne.'

EASTBOURNE. MEAD'S ROAD.

21   Paradise Drive circa 1906. Sometimes known merely as Paradise, this wonderfully named feature of the town received its title after Lady Betty Compton planted her Paradise Plantation in the grounds of Compton Place. At the same time she also erected a flint built edifice known as Ladies Bower. This is of particular interest in that it has a rare example of knapped and squared flints for wall facing. There is another example of this flint work in the wall at the entrance to Compton Place.

PARADISE DRIVE, EASTBOURNE

22 Compton Place circa 1907. It was built by James Burton in the sixteenth century and enlarged in 1730. Until 1845 it was a manor house (Bourne Place), and became the seat of the Duke of Devonshire. Royalty often stayed here, and it was a favourite spot with King George VI and his queen. She is said to have so loved the soft pink and cream of the stone-work, that she had the royal lodge at Windsor painted in similar colours. When members of the royal family visited the house, the fine chapel was in daily use.

It is now the Towner Art Gallery and Museum, still with its beautiful gardens.

Compton Place, Eastbourne.

23 Victoria Place circa 1909. The message on the postcard says: 'I am just going for a bathe. Have already used dress. Am having a splendid time. Weather is perfect.' In the picture are the Royal Victoria Baths, which were at the corner of Victoria Place and Grand Parade, so presumably this is where the writer of the card was heading. This establishment was supplied with water from the sea at every tide, and the price for the experience was one shilling for cold water, one and sixpence for hot, and three shillings for the addition of ozone. Note what appears to be a weighing machine at the entrance to the baths.

An advertisement which appeared in an 1877 Guide said: 'These baths are replete with every requisite; they have dressing rooms attached; and are conducted under the Principal's own superintendence; with Royal porcelain; fitted with all the most modern and approved appliances – their construction securing strict privacy and cleanliness. NB – Families supplied with Sea Water. Hip and other Baths on hire.'

Victoria Place, Eastbourne.

24 The attractively named Seaside Road circa 1908. The writer of the card evidently fancied himself as a humorist, as he wrote: 'It is called Seaside Road because if you look you will see a puddle, and that is where people bathe.'

The busy picture shows one of the many post offices in Eastbourne at that time. The last postal collection was around 11. p.m., and the main post office remained open each day from 7 a.m. to 10 p.m. It was of course possible to send a postcard to a friend in the morning, saying that you would be calling on them later the same day. Everyone in the picture seems to be very busy – even the dogs – although the absence of wheeled traffic is noticeable.

Eastbourne   Seaside Road

The Wrench Series No. 9763

25 'Ye Olde Lambe Hotel' in the old town. The picture is from the mid-twentieth century, although the photo has a timeless quality. (It has even been described as the oldest inn in Sussex.) This was originally a church property, used as a resting place for travelling friars, and then pilgrims, who were bound for the shrine of St. Richard. At the Reformation it was converted to an inn, later becoming a stopping place for the London coaches. Many lavish balls, lectures and local events were held here, and under the inn is an interesting vaulted chamber. In 1858 the Sussex historian Mark Antony Lower wrote that it was probably one of the oldest places of entertainment in the country. Whilst on the subject of entertainment and drink, this is a good place to mention an old Eastbourne custom known as 'Sops and Ale'. After a lady was delivered of a child, food and beer were placed in a room close to the church. After the end of the second lesson, the agricultural portion of the congregation marched out of the church and made short work of the fare provided.

26 Dormitory of St. Wini-fred's School in the early 1900s. Education was once described as Eastbourne's chief industry. Certainly there were many fine schools, most with large playing fields, particularly during the inter-war years. In 1919 it was stated that there were fifty schools for boys and almost as many for girls in the town, with perhaps as many as 2,000 boarders. A typical adver-tisement of the period spoke of 'staff of highly qualified and cultured Eng-lish and foreign mistresses, and visiting professors'. Extra care was promised for girls from India and the colonies. An exception was the school run by Thomas Hopley in the town in the 1850s. The head, although a man of several talents, was known for his belief in physical punishment of a severe kind. In 1860 he so badly beat a fifteen-year-old boy in his care that the boy later died. Hopley was charged with manslaugh-ter, and sentenced to four years in prison.

27 Water plane at Eastbourne 1900-1920. During this period the town played an interesting part in the development of aviation. The company 'Eastbourne Aviation' was founded by Frederick Bernard Fowler, with a flying school, opened in l911, and by 1912 a sea plane base. The company later made over 200 Avro fighter aircraft during the First World War. A magazine published in Eastbourne in 1914 titled 'The Visitor' (price one penny) offered a raffle with a prize of a free plane flight over Eastbourne pier. (Unfortunately the war brought an end to these flights.)

28 Great gale on 1st January 1877. Hundreds watched in amazement as the pier, which had been open for only five years, broke in the centre, with a large part disappearing beneath the waves. People hung on for dear life and were pulled to safety with difficulty. The pier lay on the sands a sorry sight and Marine Parade was described as a 'scene of desolation', with the fishermen's huts all destroyed. A man nearly lost his life dashing into the sea to save a piece of lead pipe, and others had to risk their lives to save him. Similar scenes took place all along the coast, with postcard manufacturers doing a brisk trade, commemorating the scenes with suitable views produced at very short notice.

Great Gale, 1st January 1877, Eastbourne

29 Snow storm 1908. The effects of this lasted from 28th December to mid-January. Business in Eastbourne ground to a halt and one man was driven to drink his troubles away, and laid down in the snow; having to be removed to police cells. There was a great change in the middle of January when the thaw set in with a vengeance, and the problem then became too much water.

30 The 2nd Royal Sussex Regiment Memorial Cavendish Place. As the picture shows, this was unveiled in February 1906, with a great crowd of townsfolk watching. During the period at the start of the twentieth century, such memorials became very popular, and this was a fine example. The county has always been very proud of its regiment, and in particular the Regimental March 'Sussex by the Sea' (written by Mr. W. Ward-Higgs), and first played in a concert in 1908.

31 The Tea House, Devonshire Park, circa 1930s. This was the Indian Pavilion, opened in 1875, a year after the park had been opened to the public 'for high class recreation'. Admission to the park and its twelve acres was sixpence in the afternoons and one shilling in the evenings. One of the attractions in the Tea House was Madame de Lacey with her Scientific Hand Reading. She advertised: 'Advice given on vocations and life's problems.' During the thirties there were many concerts in the park, and the very popular 'Thés dansants' thrice weekly. The Theatre was opened in 1884, and featured 'the best touring companies', and the municipal orchestra. Other events included firework displays, which in 1899 included a representation of a hive with the bees flying in and out, and a family of elephants, which were apparently made to walk. However, a newspaper reported that the beauty of the set pieces was hidden to a large extent by the masses of smoke, which the wind would persist in blowing towards the spectators.

75   EASTBOURNE. — Devonshire Park. — Tea House. — LL.

32 This is a postcard from the early part of the twentieth century, a little daring for Eastbourne, but obviously much to the taste of the sender. Almost certainly the same picture would have been used for several seaside resorts, with the name being altered on the signpost as required. The very well dressed couple show us how our grandparents went about their courting.

33 The tea garden at Holywell Retreat circa 1929. 'Holywell' probably stood for 'Hollow' in Sussex dialect, rather than 'Holy'. This was a chalk pit laid out as a garden in 1905, the cost being a mere £400. In l922 it was further enhanced, and became Holywell Italian Gardens.

In the earlier period when it was a chalk quarry, a large number of the male population of Eastbourne would have been employed here, with 3,000 loads a year being shipped to places such as Hastings and Rye.

Holywell Tea Chalet, Eastbourne

34 Proclamation of the accession of King George V at Eastbourne 1910 (although the postcard still bears an Edward Vll stamp). Before the advent of radio and TV, news of national as well as local importance would have been announced in this way, more often than not on the steps of the Town Hall. Those who were not present would then carry the information to their friends and neighbours.

35 Ward in All Saints' Hospital about 1907. This well loved convalescent hospital took its name from All Saints' Church, in Cavendish Square, London, and the organization 'The Sisters of the Community of All Saints' was responsible for its upkeep, with the support of voluntary contributions. Included in the hospital buildings was the beautiful chapel in Gothic style, which cost £19,000 to construct.

ALL SAINTS' HOSPITAL, EASTBOURNE

36 Parish Church of St. Mary the Virgin. The picture is from about 1906 and also shows the local Bobby. The church is believed to be on the site of a Saxon church, which was dedicated to St. Michael. An old tithe barn stood to the north of the church until early in the twentieth century. In 1638 Richard Vernon – vicar of Eastbourne for fifty years – was buried here at the age of 84. He had married twice, and his will asked that he be buried 'as near to my loving wives as may be'.

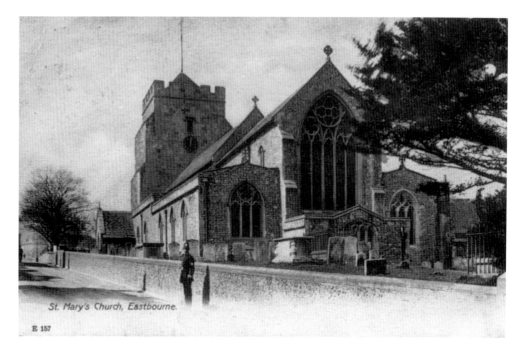

St. Mary's Church, Eastbourne.

E 157

37 The Town Hall as shown on a circa 1900 print. This is on the site of the original parish stocks, and after two years of building, it was officially opened on 20th December 1886. The total cost was £35,000 although this did not include the fittings which added a further £19,000 (the clock had to be added later). We are told that the band played Handel's Hallelujah chorus at the opening ceremony.

38 Lifeboat and Lifeboat House pictured about 1905. Eastbourne's first lifeboat was provided by the Sussex 'character' Jack Fuller of Rose Hill. When Jack died in 1833 he left the lifeboat to 'the inhabitants of Eastbourne'. In 1898 a boathouse was built, with the Duchess of Devonshire laying the foundation stone. This was followed by a further boathouse in 1902. The boat shown in this picture, one of many which served over the years, is the 'James Stevens No. 6'.

Eastbourne.   Life Boat House.

970.

39   Launching the lifeboat 'The Olive' about 1910. Martin Graebe was kind enough to send me part of the words of a song, which was sung by his grandfather each year at Christmas family gatherings in Eastbourne:

On the 14th of December,
in Eighteen Ninety-Four.
A great big ship went
and got itself wrecked,
down by the Holywell Shore.

They came down in their trousers,
their shirts and nothing more.
Got in that boat and put to sea,
and brought them safe to shore.

For seven poor souls were landed,
and all they got was wet.
If it had not been for the lifeboat
    crew,
what a watery grave they'd have
    met.

Martin is unsure of the dates in the song, and in fact these do not seem to tally with possible wrecks. But what a wonderful piece of family social history such a song represents!

LAUNCHING THE LIFEBOAT, EASTBOURNE

40 Eastbourne Railway Station from a print about 1900. The first station, which was known as Willingdon, was a very modest affair; the building shown here is the much grander station of 1886-1888. The railway had come to the town in 1849 when a four-and-a-half-mile stretch of line was opened from Polegate, with Eastbourne being described as a 'village'. The first train into the station was greeted by the band playing 'Behold the conquering hero comes'.

41   The first train into Eastbourne. This is how the magazine The Gentlewoman, in October 1915, recalled the sight of the 1849 train arriving. Only a little over half a century had elapsed, but nostalgia had already got to work on how travellers were catered for in the middle of the previous century.

42 Eastbourne Railway Station around 1906-1907. The line from Brighton to Hastings was completed in 1846, but Eastbourne passengers for London still had to go by horse bus to Polegate to get a connection. But by the beginning of the new century things were changing rapidly, and in 1935 the Southern Railway inaugurated an electric service from Eastbourne to London.

43 Hastings tram in the 1950s. Unlike some of its neighbours, Eastbourne resolutely ignored trams as a means of public transport, during the heyday of this type of travel. It was not until 1954, when most public service trams were being thought of as out of date, that the town had its first taste of this means of transport, when a narrow-gauge tramway was built for the enjoyment of visitors. The trams were one-third usual size, and the mayor drove the first tram containing local dignitaries; the event being seen on BBC tv.

44 Eastbourne lady cyclist in 1899. This is an advertisement by Alfred Cooper of Terminus Road, showing how the smart lady cyclist was dressed at that time. Great care had to be taken that too much leg was not disclosed – even to the extent of having small lead weights sewn around the bottom of the skirt, to prevent it riding up. Eastbourne had a thriving bicycle club at this time, with a newspaper report speaking of a successful outing to Horeham Road, with a return at 10. p.m.

THE " COOPER " CYCLING SKIRT.

PROV. PAT. 12379.

NO OPENINGS.

MODERATE IN PRICE.

NO VERTICAL OPENINGS WHATEVER.

Entirely closed from Waist to bottom, yet easy to get on and off. Indistinguishable for a Walking Skirt when off machine.

Sole Makers:

ALFRED COOPER

Ladies' and Gentlemen's Tailor,

126, Terminus Rd., Eastbourne

17

45 Lady's fashions in Eastbourne in 1931. This is an advertisement from a programme of a concert by the Municipal Orchestra, in Devonshire Park Floral Hall. This was of course in the days when such adverts for fur and fur-trimmed coats were quite acceptable to popular taste. The price of the coat is in guineas, which somehow made the amount seem a little less than it really was. Other advertisements in the programme were of Madame De Lacey, who offered 'Scientific Hand Reading'; the Violet Tea Rooms which offered hand-made chocolates made on the premises; and the Gondola Old-World Tea Gardens and Fishing Lake at Pevensey (bus and train service to the door).

46 The Olympian Concert Party, 1913. No seaside pier could be considered complete without its visiting Concert Party at this time. This group, led by Harry King, also included Harry Jackson, Ernest Pitt, Dorothy Eales, Franklyn Vernon and Charles Hawthorne. They all wore the almost obligatory pierrot costume, with the postcard being given away as an advertisement for the show.

THE OLYMPIAN CONCERT PARTY. THE PIER, EASTBOURNE. 1913.

HARRY KING

HARRY JACKSON   ERNEST PITT   DOROTHY EALES   FRANKLYN VERNON   CHARLES HAWTHORNE

47 The Tivoli Cinema, Seaside Road, in the 1970s. Seat prices at this time would have been about one and ninepence upwards. Like most cinemas it had experienced a varied career – first as The New Hall at the end of the nineteenth century, then around 1906 it became The New Picture Hall. By about 1912 it was known as The Eastbourne Cinema Picture Palace, with free sweets and oranges at the end of the performances. By June 1915 it was The Tivoli Cinema, with 'Super' being added to its title in 1924. After the period of this photo, it became an arts centre, a night club, and then a leisure centre, with the exterior remaining essentially unaltered.

48 This was once The Regal Cinema in Seaside, which started life as The Eastern Cinema in March 1912 with the film Vanity Fair. It then became The New Eastern Cinema in 1930, with the first talkie showing of Blackmail. It closed due to enemy action in September 1940. re-opening as The Regal Cinema in 1945. It finally closed in 1953, and by 1955 had become a branch of Woolworths, although the distinctive twin towers remained.

49   Salvation Army band about 1939. The Sally-Anns played in many venues including the beach, although a particularly popular spot was the drinking fountain, near Leaf Hall in Seaside. The early days for the Salvationists and their bands were very difficult, with their meetings and band performances being marred by violence and bitter debate, and the army's stance on drink being hotly resisted. Mobs of over 7,000 turned out, resulting in many injuries and arrests. The Town Council tried hard to prevent the Salvation Army and its bands from processing in the streets, but in the end wiser decisions prevailed, and intolerance gave way to a more kindly outlook.

50 Westminster Dragoons Camp, Eastbourne 1904. Many army camps have been held on the Downs near Eastbourne over the years; the fresh air and sunshine of this area of Sussex being much appreciated. This picture appears to be of a typical open-air church service on a Sunday morning. The message on the card says: 'Having a grand time – sleeping under canvas.'

Westminster Dragoons, I. Y.   Eastbourne, 1904.

51 Ivernia Gardens Convalescent Camp, Eastbourne in 1914-1918. Many thousands of wounded soldiers at the time of the Great War ended up at Eastbourne for rest and recuperation. The 'Blue Boys' as they were known were a familiar sight in the town, when they were able to spend some time away from their wooden huts. Among the visitors to the camps were King George V and Queen Mary.

After the war many of the wooden huts were used for temporary housing.

S 13382   "IVERNIA GARDENS" CONVALESCENT CAMP, EASTBOURNE.

52 Holidaymakers at The Angles Private Hotel, Eastbourne circa 1922. This popular hotel on Royal Parade had rooms for two hundred guests in 120 bedrooms. About this time the terms would have been around three pounds a week. Later the hotel was renamed The Majestic.

53 Another group of holidaymakers, this time in August 1939, showing very well how leisure dress changed in just a short time. This is a Methodist Church Guild Holiday at The Links, Eastbourne, just as the clouds of war were gathering, to make such carefree holidays impossible for several years. Methodist Guilds continue to exist throughout the country, and perhaps some of the young people in this picture are still members.

54 The Seaside Girl circa 1906. Although Eastbourne was noted for its splendid dress code, there were the odd exceptions. This was one, a lady who became well known around the beach area for her strange attire. The message on the back of the card says it all: 'Don't you think she looks dreadful. She goes about worse than this, and she is a lady with plenty of money.' Evidently she had enough money to indulge her taste for the bizarre, and what would any sea-side beach be without the occasional 'character'.

55 A contrast to the previous picture. Still the 1900s, but two well-dressed and suitably demure waitresses at The Imperial Restaurant, Seaside Road. Surely tea must have tasted particularly sweet when delivered by two such finely attired young ladies.

56 Fox Hunters at Compton Place around 1906. This was the East Sussex Hunt although there were also The Southdown Foxhounds. Early in this century it was reported 'foxes are not scarce'. In 1903 The Eastbourne Master was Colonel Cardwell, with kennels in the Old Town, and Hunting Days Tuesdays and Saturdays. In 1779 it was noted that there had been an astonishing run by the Eastbourne Fox Hounds of around forty miles, when the poor quarry was finally exhausted.

Eastbourne.

Compton Place.

1191

57 Universal Carrying Company vehicles. A photo of circa 1913 with my wife's father Percy Henry Godsmark (second from left) aged about 22. The company was based at 28 Junction Road, Eastbourne, with Manager E. Taylor. The company described themselves on their publicity as 'Railway and Town carriers – Collections and deliveries all over the world'. Mr. Godsmark left their employ in 1914 with a reference that stated that he was 'a good and careful driver of their 5 ton Foden Steam Wagon'.

58 Carting hay on the East Sussex Downs, near Beachy Head, in the early 1900s. Prior to the First World War, agriculture was one of the main occupations in coastal Sussex (the others being fishing, and probably smuggling). Eastbourne was noted for its annual Cattle Fair on 11th October.

Carting Hay on the Sussex Downs, near Beachy Head

59 Sheep in Gildridge Park circa 1903. (The park had been purchased for the town at around this period.) Sussex was once noted for its sheep, and the special flavour of Southdown mutton. Some believed that the small snails found only on the Downs had a lot to do with the flavour, although others said it was the wild thyme. Eastbourne was said to be the best place to catch wheatears (once a great delicacy). Sussex Downland shepherds would add to their income by catching the tiny birds in snares, and then selling them.

60 The Wilmington Gardens Wishing Well. In the early 1900s a trip from Eastbourne to the Gardens (proprietor Mr. Ebenezer) was an absolute 'must' for holidaymakers, as the trip only took about six minutes. Once there, the Wishing Well enchanted with its message:

If over me your wishes make.
Think not of glamour's fickle fate.
A simple wish for grace invoke.
When 'Wishing Well' for all good
folk.

An interesting use of the word 'glamour', which is usually thought of as a modern term.

61 Wilmington Priory
and church of St. Mary and
St. Peter about 1907. The
Priory was founded originally in the twelveth cen-
tury. It was suppressed in
1414 and subsequently fell
into ruins. It is now owned
by the Sussex Archaeo-
logical Trust.
The church claimed to
have one of the oldest yew
trees in the country (a
claim probably disputed by
several other churches). A
ghost of a peg-legged sail-
or was once said to be seen
regularly, smoking his
pipe, in the village street.

Wilmington.

Gateway of Priory and Church.

1122

62 The Wilmington Giant about 1924. This is a famous 226-ft-high figure cut into the turf on Windover Hill. His date of origin is not known, and many legends and stories surround him. One of the best-known stories is of two giants who fought each other, with the one remaining being the victor (Unlike the Cerne Giant in Dorset he is sexless). Also in this picture may be seen a team of oxen, animals which were once used by farmers regularly in this part of Sussex. There is some doubt as to which was the last team in regular use. It may have been Mr. Gorringe's team at Exceat, or Major Harding's beasts of Birling Manor farm, who were still working at East Dean in 1924. (A penny postcard was once sold at the village store showing what was claimed to be the last team.)

Wilmington Giant, near Eastbourne

63 The Tiger Inn, East Dean about 1905. (There are two East Deans in Sussex, this, and one in West Sussex.) This is a charming village, four miles from Eastbourne. The Tiger Inn, part of a row of flint buildings, was once the barracks of the local militia, although it also has many stories of smugglers and their exploits. William Bardolf had a licence to hold a weekly market here in the 13th and 14th centuries, but the Bardolf coat of arms included a leopard, so perhaps the tiger was a mistake! Parson Jonathan Darby was the vicar here in the eighteenth century, and achieved local fame by hollowing out a hole in the cliffs, from which he shone a light on stormy nights, as a refuge for ships in distress.

Ye Olde Tiger Inn, East Dean.

64 Hampden Park around 1909. What the message on a postcard described as 'a sweet little park' was nearly 100 acres, north of Eastbourne, near Willingdon. It was purchased for £3,000 on behalf of the town in 1901, and opened by Lord Rosebery in the following year. The lake shown in the photo was known originally as 'Old Decoy' but was later renamed 'Heron's Pool', when it was enlarged.

65 Willingdon village, near Eastbourne, early in the twentieth century. A timeless picture by a local photographer Percy Willby. The Well House here is notable for the knuckle-bones of sheep built into the wall. George Orwell wrote 'Animal Farm' (1945) near here. As a child he attended East-bourne College and be-longed to the Willingdon Literary Society.

66 Great Fire at Ratton Hall, Willingdon. 1892. The house was the home of Mr. Freeman-Thomas, a local landowner, and was around 100 years old. The fire was caused by an over-heated flue setting the roof alight. The mansion was completely burnt out within three hours, although the occupants escaped, and many of the valuables in the house were also saved. Two steamers and one manual fire engine came from Eastbourne, although their services were of little avail in saving the house – which lit up the country for miles around.

67   Old houses at Westham in the 1900s. This village, close to Pevensey Castle, is full of history. A Westham Curate, William Leeke, was a standard bearer at the Battle of Waterloo. He held special services for the coastguards, at odd hours, so that the smuggling gentry would not realize when no watches were being kept.

There are four 'Plague Stones' here, marking the communal grave of four victims of the epidemic of 1666.

Old Houses, Westham, Sussex. 187.

68 Pevensey Castle as seen on an old print. Originally a Roman fortress, tradition says that William landed here before the Battle of Hastings. Certainly this appears to have been the first Norman stronghold in England. In 1650 the castle was sold for £40. But in 1940 it was seen as of likely use in the event of a German invasion.

A song at the time of the threatened French invasion of England went like this:

If Bonyparte should have the heart,
to land on Pemsey Level.
Then my three sons,
with their three guns,
would blow him to the Devil.

69 Andrew Borde's bedroom in The Mint House, Pevensey. The picture is one of a set, probably from the 1930s. Andrew Borde ('Merry Andrew') was a monk and scholar who was reputed to have been born at Pevensey Vicarage early in the sixteenth century, and to have lived for some time at The Mint House. His claim to fame is his authorship of a book 'Merry Tales of the Mad Men of Gotham'. The book is full of jokes, many shaped from oral tradition. Whether Gotham was in fact a hamlet near Pevensey, or more likely a larger place of this name in Nottingham, is still in doubt. Borde died in Fleet Prison in 1549.

ANDREW BORDE'S BEDROOM, MINT HOUSE PEVENSEY

70 Railway level crossing at Polegate, a photo from the early 1900s. It was from here that the first rail line ran to Eastbourne in 1849. This was once an area of particular natural beauty, described as 'a paradise of flowers, plants, trees, animals, insects and birds'. But much of this natural scenery has now been overlaid with twentieth-century housing.

LEVEL CROSSING POLEGATE.

71 Polegate windmill. An early 20th century view. The mill was built in 1817, and with several owners it worked by wind until 1943, when electricity took over, and powered the mill until 1965. It was then purchased by the Eastbourne and District Preservation Trust; since when tremendous efforts have been made to renovate and, where necessary, rebuild the mill and its mechanism, much of the work being carried out by volunteers. The tower is 47 feet high of red brick, with the thickness of the wall varying from 2 feet 5 inches at the base, to 1 foot 4 inches at the top. Since its restoration the mill has been opened to visitors at many times during the year.

POLEGATE THE WINDMILL.   No. 11.

72 Wannock Tea Gardens, Polegate – the motor park with space for 40 chara-bancs – in the 1920s. The Gardens were opened to the public in 1927, the proud proprietor being Mr. W.J. Wootton, who claimed that the Gardens were on the site of 'the Old Original Wannock Strawberry Garden' which he said dated back two or three hundred years. The origin of the name seems to be uncertain, although it was said to be connected with the walnut trees. A guide book produced by Mr. Wootton in the 1930s, claimed that the grounds included three-and-a-half miles of walks, lily pond, 'Palm Room', 'No-Way Street', 'Boisterous Corner', 'Windy Passage' and 'Start-ler' the monkey. These names were typical of the proprietor's brand of hu-mour, exemplified in his sixpenny guide book, which ends with the mes-sage: 'Don't pass remarks about our coffee – you may be weak and old your-self someday.'

73 Beachy Head, the famous Eastbourne cliffs and beauty spot, seen on a postcard from the early 1900s. The name is said to have nothing to do with the beach, but is probably derived from the Norman 'Beau Chef'. That great country writer Richard Jefferies in one of his essays says: 'The glory of these glorious Downs is the breeze. The air in the valleys immediately beneath them is pure and pleasant; but the least climb, even a hundred feet, puts you on a plane with the atmosphere itself, uninterrupted by so much as the tree-tops.'

74   Beachy Head lighthouse in the 1900s. In July 1899 work began on the erection of the lighthouse on the foreshore under Beachy Head. The first task was to build an aerial railway from the headland. Work then continued night and day, and from a stone platform, the tower rose to a height of 120 feet. The lighthouse has seven floors, with a spiral staircase. The light came into operation on 2nd October 1902. Until the l970s electric power was from a battery charged by a wind generator, but since then power has been supplied by an 11,000-volt underground supply cable.

Beachy Head and Lighthouse, Eastbourne.

75 Belle Tout lighthouse, Beachy Head, in the early 1900s. In 1799 there was an iron cage owned by Mr. Willard of Birling farm, which was designed to draw up shipwrecked sailors from the base of the cliff by windlass and pulley. In the early part of the nineteenth century, a naval captain having escaped near disaster, wrote letters to the national press, and this resulted in a small hut being placed on Belle Tout (Belle, Bael – Celtic God of War, and Tout – old word for Look Out.) Squire Jack Fuller then paid for a permanent building in 1834 – a tower designed by William Hallett, made of Aberdeen granite, which was drawn from Maidstone by oxen. It was 47 feet high, with thirty oil lamps. The light was visible on a clear night 23 miles out to sea, but was less successful when there was a sea mist. (Experiments showed that a light near to the surface of the water worked far more efficiently.) In recent times a large part of the cliff has crashed into the sea, and this brave little lighthouse has had to be jacked-up and moved 50 feet inland.

The old Lighthouse, Beachy Head. 092

76 S.S. Eastfield stranded close to Beachy Head in December 1909 – not the first ship to come to grief at this spot. In fact this vessel was joined by a German submarine, which may be seen on other pictures from the same period. Beachy Head is noted for its outstanding natural beauty, but equally for the many dangers, which feature in so much of the history of this famous beauty spot.

S.S. EASTFIELD STRANDED AT BEACHY HEAD DEC 09